Optimizing Your Content for Voice Search Playbook

Mastering Voice Search Content Optimization

HARRELL HOWARD

Table Of Contents

Introduction — 6
Chapter 1: The Voice Search Terrain — 8
    Voice Assistants and Their Market Share — 8
    Types of Voice Search Queries — 11
    User Behavior and Expectations for Voice Search — 14
Chapter 2: How Voice Search Works — 17
    The Technology Behind Voice Search — 17
    Ranking Factors for Voice Search Results — 21
Chapter 3: Keyword Research for Voice Search — 28
    Identifying Voice Search Queries — 28
    Long-Tail Keywords and Conversational Phrases — 32
    Keyword Research Tools and Techniques — 34
Chapter 4: Content Structure and Formatting — 39
    Structuring Content for Voice Search — 39
    Using Structured Data and Schema Markup — 43
    Optimizing for Featured Snippets and Knowledge Panels — 45
Chapter 5: Writing for Voice Search — 52
    Understanding Natural Language and Conversational Tone — 52
    Crafting Concise and Direct Answers — 55
    Incorporating Questions and Commands — 58
Chapter 6: Technical Optimization — 64
    Site Speed and Mobile-Friendliness — 64
    Voice Search and Local SEO — 68
    Optimizing for Different Voice Assistants — 71
Chapter 7: Integrating Voice Search into Your Content Strategy — 78
    Identifying Voice Search Opportunities — 78
    Creating a Voice Search Content Plan — 83
    Measuring and Tracking Voice Search Performance — 88

Chapter 8: Voice Search and Emerging Technologies — **94**
    Voice Search and the Internet of Things (IoT) — 94
    Voice Commerce and Voice Shopping — 98
    Artificial Intelligence and Voice Search Evolution — 103

Conclusion — **110**
    Recap of Key Points — 110
    Future of Voice Search and Content Optimization — 113
    Final Thoughts and Recommendations — 116
    Resources — 118

Introduction

What is voice search?

Voice search is a technology that allows users to search the internet, control devices, and perform various tasks by speaking into a voice-enabled device, such as a smartphone, smart speaker, or virtual assistant. This technology utilizes natural language processing (NLP) and speech recognition to understand the user's spoken query and provide a relevant response.

The rise of voice search and its importance

The use of voice search has been rapidly increasing in recent years, driven by the widespread adoption of voice-enabled devices and the growing preference for hands-free, conversational search experiences. According to industry reports, the global voice search market is expected to reach over $30 billion by 2027, with a compound annual growth rate (CAGR) of more than 20% from 2022 to 2027.

Why optimizing for voice search is crucial

As voice search continues to gain popularity, it is becoming increasingly important for businesses and content creators to optimize their content for this growing search channel. Voice search optimization can help improve the discoverability and accessibility of your content, leading to increased traffic, engagement, and potential conversions. Additionally, by catering to the unique behaviors and expectations of voice search users, you can provide a more seamless and satisfactory user experience, which can positively impact your overall digital marketing strategy.

Chapter 1: The Voice Search Terrain

Voice Assistants and Their Market Share

The voice search terrain is dominated by a handful of key players, each with its own unique features, capabilities, and market share. Understanding the leading voice assistants and their respective positions in the market is crucial for optimizing your content for the most relevant platforms.

Amazon Alexa

Amazon's Alexa is one of the most widely adopted voice assistants, with a significant market share in the smart speaker and broader voice assistant domains. Alexa is the default voice assistant for Amazon's Echo line of smart speakers, as well as many other Alexa-enabled devices. Alexa's strengths include its extensive skills and integrations, natural language understanding, and robust knowledge base, making it a popular choice for a wide range of voice-based tasks, from information lookup to smart home control and voice commerce.

Google Assistant

Google Assistant, developed by tech giant Google, is another major player in the voice search terrain. Integrated into Android devices, Google search, and the company's own Google Home smart speakers, Google Assistant leverages Google's vast knowledge and data to provide comprehensive and accurate voice-based responses. Its key advantages include seamless integration with Google's ecosystem, advanced natural language processing, and the ability to understand and respond to complex queries.

Apple Siri

Apple's Siri is the voice assistant built into iOS devices, macOS computers, and the company's HomePod smart speakers. Siri is known for its strong integration with Apple's hardware and software ecosystem, as well as its emphasis on privacy and security. While Siri's capabilities have expanded over the years, it still trails behind Alexa and Google Assistant in overall functionality and market share, particularly in the smart speaker segment.

Microsoft Cortana

Microsoft Cortana is the voice assistant developed by the tech giant Microsoft. Cortana is integrated into Windows devices, as well as some third-party smart speakers and other products. Cortana's strengths include its integration with Microsoft's productivity suite, such as Outlook and Office 365, as well as its ability to handle complex queries and tasks. However, Cortana has a relatively smaller market share compared to the leading voice assistants, particularly in the consumer-facing smart speaker and home automation domains.

Understanding the market share and unique capabilities of these major voice assistants is essential for optimizing your content for voice search. By tailoring your content and strategies to the specific requirements and strengths of the dominant voice assistants, you can increase the visibility and relevance of your content in voice search results.

Types of Voice Search Queries

Voice search queries can be categorized into different types, each with its own characteristics and optimization requirements. Knowing the common types of voice search queries can help you align your content and targeting strategies to better address the needs and expectations of voice search users.

Informational Queries

Informational queries are the most common type of voice search, where users are seeking factual information, answers to questions, or general knowledge. These queries often begin with words like "what," "who," "when," "where," or "how," and require concise and direct responses. Examples include "What is the capital of France?" or "How tall is the Eiffel Tower?"

Navigational Queries

Navigational queries are used when the user is looking for a specific website, brand, or online destination. These queries typically involve the name of the entity the user is seeking, such as "Amazon" or "Wikipedia." Optimizing for navigational queries often involves ensuring your brand name and website are accurately represented in voice search results.

Transactional Queries

Transactional queries are associated with the user's intent to perform a specific action, such as making a purchase, booking a reservation, or completing a transaction. These queries may include words like "buy," "order," "book," or "reserve," and require optimization that supports seamless voice-based interactions and transactions.

Local Queries

Local queries are those where the user is seeking information or services in their immediate geographic area, such as finding the nearest restaurant, store, or service provider. These queries often include location-based keywords, such as a city or neighborhood name, or phrases like "near me" or "in [location]." Optimizing for local voice search queries involves leveraging local SEO strategies and ensuring your business information is accurately represented across various platforms.

Understanding the different types of voice search queries and their unique characteristics is crucial for developing a comprehensive voice search optimization strategy. By aligning your content and targeting efforts to the specific needs and expectations of each query type, you can improve the visibility, relevance, and performance of your content in voice search results.

User Behavior and Expectations for Voice Search

Voice search users tend to exhibit distinct behaviors and have unique expectations compared to traditional text-based search. Recognizing these differences is essential for effective voice search optimization.

Conversational and Natural Language

One of the defining characteristics of voice search is the use of more conversational and natural language. Users tend to speak their queries in a more natural, conversational tone, often using complete sentences and phrases that mirror how they would ask a question or make a request in person. This contrasts with the more concise, keyword-driven queries typically used in text-based searches.

Desire for Concise and Direct Answers

Voice search users typically have a lower tolerance for lengthy, multi-paragraph responses. They expect concise, direct, and actionable answers to their queries. Voice search results need to provide the most relevant and pertinent information in a succinct, easy-to-digest format, often in the form of a featured snippet or a short, summarized response.

Expectation of Personalization and Seamlessness

Voice search users expect a highly personalized and seamless experience. They anticipate that the voice assistant will understand their context, preferences, and intent, and provide tailored responses and recommendations. This level of personalization and responsiveness is a key factor in shaping user expectations and satisfaction with voice search experiences.

Reliance on Hands-Free and Mobile Interactions

Voice search is inherently a hands-free, mobile-driven experience. Users often engage with voice search while on the go, multitasking, or in situations where traditional text-based search is less convenient or practical. This reliance on hands-free, mobile interactions shapes the user's expectations for speed, accessibility, and seamless integration with their devices and daily routines.

Understanding these unique user behaviors and expectations is crucial for optimizing your content and strategies for voice search. By aligning your content and experiences to address the needs and preferences of voice search users, you can enhance the discoverability, relevance, and overall performance of your content in the voice search terrain.

Chapter 2: How Voice Search Works

The Technology Behind Voice Search

The technology that powers voice search is a complex and dynamic ecosystem, leveraging a combination of natural language processing (NLP), speech recognition, and machine learning algorithms. These technologies work together seamlessly to enable users to search, interact, and retrieve information using their voice.

Natural Language Processing (NLP)

At the heart of voice search technology is natural language processing (NLP), a field of artificial intelligence that focuses on the interaction between computers and human language. NLP enables voice search systems to understand the semantic meaning, intent, and context behind a user's spoken query, allowing them to provide relevant and meaningful responses.

The NLP process typically involves several key steps:

1. **Speech-to-Text Conversion**: The first step in the NLP process is to convert the user's spoken query into a machine-readable text format. This is achieved through advanced speech recognition algorithms that analyze the audio input and transcribe it into written text.
2. **Linguistic Analysis**: Once the spoken query has been converted to text, the NLP system analyzes the linguistic structure, syntax, and semantics of the query. This involves breaking down the text into individual words, understanding the relationships between them, and identifying the overall meaning and intent behind the query.
3. **Intent Extraction**: NLP algorithms then work to extract the user's intent from the query, determining what the user is

seeking to accomplish or learn. This understanding of intent is crucial for retrieving the most relevant information or taking the appropriate actions in response to the query.
4. **Context Interpretation**: Voice search systems also leverage NLP to interpret the context surrounding the user's query, such as their location, search history, or device information. This contextual understanding helps to personalize the response and provide more accurate and tailored results.

Speech Recognition

Speech recognition is the other key technology that enables voice search. This process involves converting the user's spoken words into a machine-readable format that can be processed and understood by the voice search system.

Speech recognition systems typically employ a combination of acoustic modeling and language modeling to accurately transcribe speech. Acoustic modeling analyzes the audio input to identify individual speech sounds, while language modeling leverages statistical and linguistic knowledge to predict the most likely words and phrases based on the context.

Advanced speech recognition algorithms, powered by deep learning and neural networks, have significantly improved the accuracy and robustness of voice-to-text conversion in recent years, making voice search a more reliable and user-friendly experience.

Machine Learning and Artificial Intelligence

Underpinning the natural language processing and speech recognition technologies are sophisticated machine learning and artificial intelligence (AI) algorithms. These algorithms enable voice search systems to continuously learn, adapt, and improve their performance over time, based on user interactions and feedback.

Through the application of machine learning techniques, such as deep learning, voice search systems can better understand the nuances of human language, recognize and respond to complex queries, and provide increasingly personalized and relevant results. As the volume of voice search data grows, these AI-powered systems become more accurate and effective at understanding and interpreting users' spoken queries.

The integration of these core technologies – natural language processing, speech recognition, and machine learning – is what enables voice search to function as a seamless, intuitive, and powerful search and interaction modality for users.

Ranking Factors for Voice Search Results

While voice search shares some similarities with traditional text-based search in terms of ranking factors, there are several unique considerations that come into play when determining the most relevant and optimal voice search results.

Conciseness and Directness

One of the primary differentiating factors for voice search is the emphasis on conciseness and directness in the search results. Voice search users typically expect to receive a succinct, straightforward answer to their query, rather than a lengthy, multi-paragraph response. Search engines, therefore, prioritize content that can provide a clear, concise, and direct answer to the user's question.

Relevance and Contextual Understanding

Relevance is always a key factor in search, but in the context of voice search, the search engine's ability to understand the user's intent and the context of the query becomes even more critical. Voice search systems must be able to accurately interpret the meaning and purpose behind the user's spoken query, and then retrieve the most relevant and useful information to address their needs.

Ability to Provide a Featured Snippet

Featured snippets, also known as "answer boxes," are a particularly important ranking factor for voice search. These concise, directly-answered excerpts of content are often read aloud by voice assistants as the featured response to a user's query. Optimizing your content to be selected as a featured snippet can significantly improve its chances of being the chosen voice search result.

Structured Data and Schema Markup

The use of structured data and schema markup can also play a significant role in voice search ranking. By providing search engines with clear, machine-readable information about the content and context of your web pages, you can enhance their ability to understand and properly display your content in voice search results, including as featured snippets or knowledge panels.

Mobile-Friendliness and Page Speed

Given the inherent mobile nature of voice search, factors such as mobile-friendliness and page speed are also crucial ranking signals. Voice search users expect a seamless, responsive experience, and search engines will prioritize content that loads quickly and provides a positive user experience on mobile devices.

Local Relevance and Entity Understanding

For certain types of voice search queries, such as those related to local businesses or services, search engines place a high emphasis on the local relevance and entity understanding of the content. Optimizing your content for local SEO, including accurate and comprehensive business listings, can improve its visibility in voice search results for location-based queries.

Understanding these unique ranking factors for voice search and aligning your content optimization strategies accordingly can significantly enhance the discoverability and performance of your content in the voice search terrain.

The technology behind voice search is a complex and dynamic ecosystem, leveraging a combination of natural language processing (NLP), speech recognition, and machine learning algorithms. These technologies work together to enable users to search, interact, and retrieve information using their voice.

NLP is the core technology that enables voice search systems to understand and interpret human language, analyzing the semantic meaning, syntax, and context of the spoken query. Speech recognition, on the other hand, is the process of converting the user's spoken words into a machine-readable text format.

Underlying these technologies are sophisticated machine learning and artificial intelligence (AI) algorithms, which enable voice search systems to continuously learn, adapt, and improve their performance over time, based on user interactions and feedback.

The ranking factors for voice search results differ from traditional text-based search, with an emphasis on factors such as conciseness, relevance, the ability to provide a direct answer, structured data and schema markup, mobile-friendliness, page speed, and local relevance. Understanding these unique ranking factors and aligning your content optimization strategies accordingly can significantly enhance the discoverability and performance of your content in the voice search terrain.

By leveraging the power of natural language processing, speech recognition, and machine learning, voice search technology has become a transformative force in the way users interact with and retrieve information. As the technology continues to evolve, understanding the inner workings of voice search will be crucial for content creators and businesses to stay ahead of the curve and optimize their content for this rapidly growing search channel.

Chapter 3: Keyword Research for Voice Search

Identifying Voice Search Queries

Effective voice search optimization starts with identifying the types of queries that your target audience is likely to use when engaging with voice search. This involves conducting thorough keyword research to uncover the common voice search phrases, long-tail keywords, and conversational queries related to your business or industry.

Understanding User Intent and Search Behavior

The first step in identifying voice search queries is to gain a deep understanding of your target audience's intent and search behavior. Consider the types of questions, commands, or informational needs that your audience is likely to have and how they might express those needs using voice search.

Some key factors to consider when analyzing user intent and search behavior for voice search include:

1. **Common Information Needs**: What type of information are your users typically seeking, such as product details, business hours, directions, or general knowledge?
2. **Conversational Phrasing**: How might your users phrase their queries in a more natural, conversational tone compared to text-based search?
3. **Device Usage**: How and where are your users likely to engage with voice search, such as on a smart speaker, smartphone, or other connected device?
4. **User Context**: What contextual factors, such as location, time of day, or previous search history, might influence the types of voice search queries your users make?

By developing a comprehensive understanding of your target audience's intent and search behavior, you can more effectively identify the specific voice search queries that are most relevant to your business or content.

Researching Common Voice Search Phrases

Once you have a solid understanding of your target audience's search behavior, you can begin researching the specific voice search phrases they are likely to use. This involves a combination of keyword research techniques, such as:

1. **Leveraging Voice Search-Specific Tools**: There are several keyword research tools that are designed specifically for voice search optimization, such as Answer the Public, which provides insights into common voice search queries based on popular questions and phrases.

2. **Analyzing Competitor Data**: Examining the voice search strategies and content of your competitors can provide valuable insights into the types of queries that are prevalent in your industry.
3. **Reviewing Internal Site Data**: If you have an existing website or online presence, you can analyze the search queries and voice-based interactions that users have had with your content to identify relevant voice search phrases.
4. **Conducting User Surveys and Interviews**: Directly engaging with your target audience through surveys or interviews can help you uncover the specific language and phrasing they use when conducting voice searches.

By combining these various research techniques, you can develop a comprehensive list of the most common and relevant voice search queries related to your business or industry.

Long-Tail Keywords and Conversational Phrases

Long-tail keywords and conversational phrases are particularly important for voice search optimization, as they tend to be more specific and closely aligned with the natural language used in voice queries.

Long-Tail Keywords

Long-tail keywords are longer, more specific search phrases that typically have lower search volume but higher relevance and conversion potential. In the context of voice search, long-tail keywords can be especially valuable, as they often mirror the way users naturally express their search queries orally.

Examples of long-tail voice search keywords include:

- "What is the best hiking trail near me?"
- "How to make homemade chocolate chip cookies"

- "Directions to the nearest coffee shop"

By incorporating these types of long-tail keywords into your content, you can improve the visibility and relevance of your content in voice search results, as they are more closely aligned with the specific information needs and search behavior of your target audience.

Conversational Phrases

In addition to long-tail keywords, it is equally important to identify and incorporate conversational phrases into your voice search optimization strategy. Conversational phrases are the natural, colloquial language that users employ when conducting voice searches, often in the form of questions or commands.

Examples of conversational voice search phrases include:

- "Who is the current president of the United States?"
- "Show me the nearest Italian restaurant"

- "How do I change a flat tire on my car?"

These types of conversational phrases tend to be more natural, contextual, and closely aligned with the way users actually speak and formulate their queries. By optimizing your content to address these conversational phrases, you can enhance its discoverability and relevance in voice search results.

Keyword Research Tools and Techniques

There are a variety of keyword research tools and techniques that can be leveraged to identify and optimize for voice search queries. These include both generic keyword research tools, as well as those specifically designed for voice search optimization.

Voice Search-Specific Tools

Some of the key voice search-specific keyword research tools include:

1. **Answer the Public**: This tool analyzes search engine autocomplete data to provide insights into the types of questions and phrases users are searching for, including many that arc specifically tailored for voice search.
2. **Backlinko Voice Search Analyzer**: Backlinko's free tool allows you to analyze the voice search performance of any webpage, providing detailed data on the types of queries the content is ranking for.
3. **Moz Keyword Explorer**: Moz's Keyword Explorer includes features specifically designed for voice search optimization, including the ability to identify long-tail and conversational keywords.
4. **Yoast Voice Search Optimization**: The Yoast SEO plugin for WordPress includes a voice search optimization module, which provides guidance on optimizing content for voice search.

Leveraging Competitor and Internal Data

In addition to voice search-specific tools, you can also leverage other keyword research techniques to inform your voice search optimization strategy, such as:

1. **Competitor Analysis**: Analyzing the voice search strategies and content of your competitors can provide valuable insights into the types of queries they are targeting and how you can differentiate your own approach.
2. **Internal Search Data**: If you have an existing website or online presence, reviewing the search queries and voice-based interactions that users have had with your content can help you identify relevant voice search phrases.
3. **Customer Interviews and Surveys**: Directly engaging with your target audience through interviews or surveys can help you uncover the specific language and phrasing they use when conducting voice searches.

By combining the insights from these various keyword research tools and techniques, you can develop a comprehensive understanding of the voice search queries that are most relevant to your business or content, and then optimize your strategies accordingly.

Effective voice search optimization starts with identifying the types of queries that your target audience is likely to use. This involves a multi-faceted approach to keyword research, including understanding user intent and search behavior, researching common voice search phrases, and leveraging long-tail keywords and conversational phrases.

Long-tail keywords and conversational phrases are particularly important for voice search optimization, as they tend to be more specific and closely aligned with the natural language used in voice queries. Incorporating these types of keywords into your content can significantly improve its visibility and relevance in voice search results.

To uncover these valuable voice search keywords, you can utilize a variety of research tools and techniques, including voice search-specific keyword research tools, competitor analysis, and internal search data. By combining these insights, you can develop a comprehensive understanding of the voice search queries that are most relevant to your business or content, and then optimize your strategies accordingly.

By mastering the art of voice search keyword research, you can position your content for success in the rapidly evolving voice search terrain, enhancing its discoverability, relevance, and overall performance. This, in turn, can lead to increased traffic, engagement, and potential conversions for your business or online presence.

Chapter 4: Content Structure and Formatting

Structuring Content for Voice Search

Organizing your content in a clear and concise manner is crucial for effective voice search optimization. This involves employing a well-structured and user-friendly content hierarchy, providing straightforward and direct answers, and aligning your content with the typical flow of voice search queries.

Using Relevant Headers and Subheadings

The use of clear and relevant headers and subheadings can significantly improve the structure and scanability of your content, making it easier for both users and search engines to navigate and understand. When structuring your content for voice search, pay close attention to the following:

1. **H1 (Main Heading)**: Your main heading should effectively communicate the

primary topic or focus of your content, using language that is natural and resonates with your target audience's voice search queries.

2. **H2 (Major Subheadings)**: Major subheadings should further break down your content into logical sections, with each H2 heading addressing a key subtopic or aspect of the main subject.

3. **H3 (Minor Subheadings)**: Utilize H3 subheadings to provide an even more granular level of organization, allowing you to delve deeper into specific details or concepts within each major section.

By employing a clear and intuitive hierarchy of headers, you can help voice search users quickly locate the information they need and ensure that your content is optimized for the typical flow of voice search queries.

Providing Straightforward and Direct Answers

Voice search users typically expect concise and direct answers to their queries, with little tolerance for lengthy, multi-paragraph responses. When structuring your content, focus on providing straightforward answers to the user's question or request, without extraneous information.

This may involve:

- Identifying the key facts, steps, or insights that directly address the user's query
- Presenting this information in a succinct, easy-to-digest format
- Avoiding lengthy preambles or excessive contextual details
- Prioritizing clarity and conciseness over comprehensive coverage

By structuring your content to deliver clear and direct answers, you can better meet the expectations of voice search users and increase the likelihood of your content being selected as the featured response.

Aligning with the Voice Search Query Flow

The structure of your content should also align with the typical flow and progression of voice search queries. This may involve:

1. **Anticipating Common Questions**: Organize your content to address the most common questions or informational needs that users are likely to have about your topic or subject matter.
2. **Providing Step-by-Step Guidance**: For queries involving how-to instructions or processes, structure your content in a clear, sequential manner to guide the user through the necessary steps.
3. **Incorporating Relevant Context**: Ensure that your content provides the appropriate context and background information to fully address the user's query, without overwhelming them with extraneous details.

By structuring your content to meet the expectations and flow of typical voice search queries, you can enhance the user experience and improve the overall relevance and effectiveness of your content in voice search results.

Using Structured Data and Schema Markup

Structured data and schema markup are powerful tools for improving the visibility and performance of your content in voice search results. By providing search engines with clear, machine-readable information about the content and context of your web pages, you can enhance their ability to understand and properly display your content in voice search results, including as featured snippets or knowledge panels.

Structured Data

Structured data refers to the use of standardized, machine-readable formats, such as JSON-LD, Microdata, or RDFa, to encode information about the content, entities, and relationships on your web pages. This structured data can include details about the page's author, publication date, product information, reviews, events, and more.

By incorporating structured data into your web pages, you can provide search engines with a better understanding of the content and context, which can improve the chances of your content being selected and displayed in a prominent way in voice search results.

Schema Markup

Schema markup is a specific type of structured data vocabulary developed by the major search engines (Google, Bing, Yahoo, and Yandex) to help search engines understand the meaning and context of web content. The schema.org vocabulary includes a wide range of predefined entity types and properties that you can use to markup your content, such as:

- **Organization**: Information about your business or organization
- **LocalBusiness**: Details about a local business, such as hours, location, and contact information
- **Product**: Specifications and details about a product or service
- **Review**: Ratings and reviews for a product, service, or business
- **Event**: Information about an upcoming event, such as date, time, and location

By using schema markup to annotate the relevant entities and relationships within your content, you can enhance the search engines' ability to recognize and properly display your content in voice search results, including as featured snippets or knowledge panels.

Optimizing for Featured Snippets and Knowledge Panels

Featured snippets and knowledge panels are particularly important for voice search optimization, as they provide the direct answer or information that voice search users are typically seeking. Optimizing your content to be selected as a featured snippet or knowledge panel can significantly improve your chances of being the chosen voice search result.

Featured Snippets

Featured snippets are the concise, directly-answered excerpts of content that are prominently displayed at the top of search engine results pages (SERPs). These featured snippets are often read aloud by voice assistants as the featured response to a user's query.

To optimize your content for featured snippets, consider the following strategies:

1. **Identify Relevant Question-Based Queries**: Analyze the types of questions and queries your target audience is likely to ask, and structure your content to directly address these queries.

2. **Provide Clear, Concise Answers**: Ensure that your content presents the key information or steps needed to answer the user's query in a straightforward, easy-to-understand manner.
3. **Use Structured Formatting**: Leverage clear headings, bullet points, tables, and other formatting techniques to make your content easy for search engines to parse and display as a featured snippet.
4. **Incorporate Relevant Schema Markup**: Annotate your content with appropriate schema markup, such as the "Question" and "Answer" entities, to further signal its relevance and suitability for featured snippets.

Knowledge Panels

Knowledge panels are the informative, summarized boxes that are often displayed on the right-hand side of search engine results pages, providing quick access to key facts and details about a particular entity, such as a business, person, or organization.

To optimize your content for knowledge panels, consider the following strategies:

1. **Identify Relevant Entities**: Determine the key entities (people, places, products, etc.) that are relevant to your content and ensure that they are accurately represented.
2. **Provide Comprehensive Entity Information**: Ensure that your content includes comprehensive and accurate details about the relevant entities, such as their description, location, contact information, and other pertinent facts.
3. **Use Structured Data and Schema Markup**: Annotate your content with appropriate schema markup to signal the various entities and their relationships, making it easier for search engines to understand and display the information in a knowledge panel.

4. **Ensure Data Accuracy and Consistency**: Regularly review and update your content to ensure that all entity-related information is accurate and consistent across your website and other online properties.

By optimizing your content for featured snippets and knowledge panels, you can significantly increase its visibility and relevance in voice search results, making it more likely to be selected as the featured response to a user's query.

Organizing your content in a clear and concise manner is crucial for voice search optimization. This involves using relevant headers and subheadings, providing straightforward and direct answers, and structuring your content in a way that aligns with the typical flow of voice search queries.

Structured data and schema markup can also play a crucial role in improving the visibility and relevance of your content in voice search results. By providing search engines with clear, machine-readable information about the content and context of your web pages, you can enhance their ability to understand and properly display your content, including as featured snippets or knowledge panels.

Featured snippets and knowledge panels are particularly important for voice search, as they provide the direct answer or information that voice search users are typically seeking. Optimizing your content to be selected as a featured snippet or knowledge panel can significantly improve your chances of being the chosen voice search result.

By implementing these content structure and formatting best practices, you can position your content for success in the increasingly competitive voice search terrain, improving its discoverability, relevance, and overall performance.

Chapter 5: Writing for Voice Search

Understanding Natural Language and Conversational Tone

One of the key characteristics that distinguishes voice search from traditional text-based search is the use of more conversational and natural language. Voice search queries tend to be phrased in a more natural, colloquial manner, mirroring how people would actually speak and ask questions.

When writing content for voice search optimization, it's crucial to adopt a more natural and conversational style, using language that resonates with the way your target audience would express their queries orally.

Adopting a Conversational Tone

To strike the right tone for voice search, consider the following strategies:

1. **Use Conversational Syntax**: Structure your sentences in a more natural,

conversational flow, rather than adhering to strict formal writing conventions. This may involve using shorter sentences, contractions, and rhetorical questions.

2. **Incorporate Colloquial Expressions**: Sprinkle in common colloquial expressions and idioms that reflect how people would naturally speak, such as "What's the deal with..." or "How do I go about..."

3. **Address the Reader Directly**: Use second-person pronouns like "you" and "your" to create a more personalized, conversational tone and make the content feel like a direct response to the user's query.

4. **Mimic Spoken Language**: Pay attention to the cadence, rhythm, and phrasing of spoken language, and try to capture that in your written content. This can involve using more varied sentence structures, pauses, and rhetorical devices.

By adopting a more natural, conversational tone in your writing, you can better align your content with the way users typically express themselves in voice search queries, enhancing the relevance and relatability of your content.

Considering User Context and Intent

Another key aspect of writing for voice search is understanding the user's context and intent behind their query. Voice search users often have specific goals or informational needs that may differ from those of traditional text-based searchers.

When crafting your content, consider factors such as:

1. **Device Usage**: Is the user conducting the search on a smart speaker, smartphone, or other voice-enabled device? This can influence the type of information they're seeking and the level of detail they expect.
2. **Location and Time of Day**: Where and when the user is conducting the search

may impact the relevance of certain types of information, such as nearby businesses, events, or weather-related content.
3. **User Persona and Interests**: Understanding your target audience's demographics, pain points, and interests can help you tailor the tone, language, and informational focus of your content to meet their specific needs.

By taking these contextual factors into account, you can create content that more effectively anticipates and addresses the user's underlying intent, further enhancing the relevance and usefulness of your voice search-optimized content.

Crafting Concise and Direct Answers

Voice search users typically have a lower tolerance for lengthy, multi-paragraph responses. They expect concise, direct, and actionable answers to their queries, with little patience for excessive preamble or extraneous information.

When writing content for voice search, it's crucial to focus on providing the most relevant and succinct information to address the user's needs.

Identifying the Key Information

The first step in crafting concise and direct answers is to identify the core information that the user is seeking. This may involve:

1. **Anticipating Common Questions**: Analyze the types of queries your target audience is likely to ask, and structure your content to directly address those questions.
2. **Prioritizing the Most Relevant Details**: Determine the most essential facts, steps, or insights that are directly relevant to the user's query, and present them in a focused manner.

3. **Eliminating Unnecessary Details**: Avoid including extraneous information or contextual details that don't directly contribute to answering the user's question or meeting their needs.

By honing in on the key information that the user is seeking, you can craft concise and direct answers that are well-suited for the voice search experience.

Organizing Content for Clarity

In addition to identifying the core information, it's important to structure your content in a clear and logical manner to enhance its suitability for voice search. Strategies include:

1. **Using Succinct Headings and Subheadings**: Employ clear, straightforward headers and subheadings that accurately reflect the content within each section.

2. **Presenting Information in a Step-by-Step Format**: For how-to or instructional content, organize the steps in a sequential, easy-to-follow manner.
3. **Leveraging Bullet Points and Lists**: Break down information into concise, scannable bullet points or numbered lists to make it easier for users to quickly digest.
4. **Minimizing Lengthy Paragraphs**: Avoid long, dense paragraphs in favor of shorter, more focused sentences and statements.

By organizing your content in a clear and concise manner, you can make it easier for voice search users to quickly find and comprehend the information they need, enhancing the overall user experience and the relevance of your content in voice search results.

Incorporating Questions and Commands

Another effective strategy for writing content optimized for voice search is to frame your content around the types of questions and commands that your target audience is likely to use when conducting voice searches.

Anticipating Common Questions

By anticipating the specific questions your audience is likely to ask, you can structure your content to directly address those queries in a way that aligns with the natural flow of voice search interactions.

Some examples of common question-based voice search queries include:

- "What is the weather forecast for today?"
- "How do I change a flat tire on my car?"
- "Who is the current president of the United States?"

Incorporating these types of question-based keywords and phrases into your content can improve its relevance and visibility in voice search results.

Addressing Commands and Requests

In addition to questions, voice search users often employ more direct, command-based queries to achieve specific goals or complete tasks. By structuring your content to address these types of commands, you can further enhance its suitability for voice search optimization.

Examples of command-based voice search queries include:

- "Find the nearest Italian restaurant"
- "Play my favorite song"
- "Set a timer for 30 minutes"

By anticipating and addressing these types of commands within your content, you can better align your information and guidance with the user's intent, improving the overall effectiveness of your voice search optimization efforts.

Optimizing Content Structure

To effectively incorporate questions and commands into your voice search-optimized content, consider the following structural techniques:

1. **Use Question-Based Headings**: Craft clear, question-based headers and subheadings that directly address the user's query.
2. **Provide Straightforward Answers**: Structure your content to deliver concise, directly-answered responses to the user's questions or commands.
3. **Anticipate Follow-Up Queries**: Organize your content in a way that anticipates and addresses potential follow-up questions or requests related to the initial query.

By aligning your content with the common question-based and command-based search patterns of your target audience, you can enhance the relevance and visibility of your content in voice search results, ultimately delivering a more seamless and satisfactory experience for the user.

When writing content for voice search optimization, it's crucial to adopt a more natural and conversational style, using language that mirrors how people speak and ask questions. This involves employing a conversational tone, considering the user's context and intent, and incorporating elements of natural language, such as colloquial expressions and rhetorical questions.

Voice search users typically prefer short, concise, and direct answers to their queries. To craft content that meets these expectations, focus on identifying the key information needed to address the user's needs, and organize your content in a clear and logical manner, using techniques like succinct headings, step-by-step formatting, and bullet points.

Framing your content around common voice search queries, such as questions and commands, can also help improve its relevance and visibility in voice search results. By anticipating the types of questions and commands your target audience is likely to use, and structuring your content accordingly, you can better align your information and guidance with the user's intent.

By mastering the art of writing for voice search, you can create content that not only resonates with the natural language and conversational preferences of your audience, but also delivers the concise, actionable answers they are seeking. This, in turn, can enhance the overall performance and impact of your voice search optimization efforts.

Chapter 6: Technical Optimization

Site Speed and Mobile-Friendliness

Technical factors, such as site speed and mobile-friendliness, play a crucial role in voice search optimization. Voice search users expect fast and seamless experiences, and search engines prioritize content that provides a positive user experience, especially on mobile devices.

The Importance of Site Speed

Site speed is a critical technical factor for voice search optimization. Voice search users typically expect instantaneous responses to their queries, and they have little tolerance for slow-loading web pages or content.

Several key factors contribute to the importance of site speed for voice search:

> 1. **User Experience**: Slow-loading websites can frustrate users, leading to higher bounce rates and a negative overall

experience. This is particularly detrimental in the context of voice search, where users expect a smooth and efficient interaction.

2. **Search Engine Ranking**: Search engines, such as Google, have made site speed a ranking factor, prioritizing faster-loading websites in their search results, including voice search.

3. **Mobile-Friendliness**: Voice search is predominantly a mobile-driven experience, and mobile users are even more sensitive to slow-loading content. Ensuring your website is optimized for fast loading times on mobile devices is essential for voice search performance.

To improve your site speed for voice search optimization, consider implementing strategies such as:

- Optimizing image and media files
- Minimizing the use of heavy scripts and plugins

- Leveraging content delivery networks (CDNs)
- Implementing caching techniques
- Monitoring and addressing any server-side performance issues

By prioritizing site speed, you can enhance the user experience and improve your chances of ranking well in voice search results.

The Importance of Mobile-Friendliness

In addition to site speed, mobile-friendliness is another crucial technical factor for voice search optimization. As the majority of voice searches are conducted on mobile devices, ensuring your website and content are optimized for a seamless mobile experience is essential.

Several key aspects of mobile-friendliness that are particularly important for voice search include:

1. **Responsive Design**: Your website should be designed to adapt and display correctly

across a wide range of mobile devices and screen sizes, providing a consistent and user-friendly experience.
2. **Touch-Friendly Interactions**: Ensure that your website's navigation, content, and calls-to-action are easy to interact with on a touchscreen, with appropriately sized and spaced elements.
3. **Simplified Content Structure**: Organize your content in a way that is easily digestible and scannable on a mobile device, with clear headings, short paragraphs, and concise information.
4. **Reduced Content Load Times**: Optimize your mobile pages for faster loading times, as mentioned in the previous section, to provide a smooth and responsive experience for voice search users.

By addressing these mobile-friendliness factors, you can create a more user-friendly experience for voice search users, which can positively impact your visibility and performance in voice search results.

Voice Search and Local SEO

Local SEO is particularly important for voice search, as many voice queries are related to finding local businesses, services, or information. Optimizing your content and website for local search can significantly improve your visibility and relevance in voice search results.

The Rise of Local Voice Search

As voice search continues to grow in popularity, an increasing number of voice queries are focused on local information, such as the nearest restaurant, store, or service provider. This is driven by several factors:

1. **Mobile Usage**: The majority of voice searches are conducted on mobile devices, which often have a strong association with local intent and context.

2. **Convenience and Immediacy**: Voice search users frequently seek information or solutions that are immediately accessible and relevant to their current location and needs.
3. **Adoption of Voice Assistants**: The widespread adoption of voice assistants, such as Alexa, Siri, and Google Assistant, has led to an increase in local-focused queries, as users leverage these tools to find nearby businesses and services.

By understanding the rising importance of local voice search, businesses and content creators can tailor their optimization strategies to better meet the needs of this growing segment of voice search users.

Optimizing for Local Voice Search

To optimize your content and website for local voice search, consider the following strategies:

1. **Claim and Optimize Your Business Listings**: Ensure that your business information, including your name, address, phone number, and website, is accurately listed and optimized across various local directories and search platforms.
2. **Leverage Location-Based Keywords**: Incorporate relevant location-based keywords, such as your city, neighborhood, or region, into your content to signal the local relevance of your offerings.
3. **Provide Detailed Local Information**: Include detailed information about your business's location, hours of operation, services, and other relevant details that can help voice search users find and engage with your offerings.
4. **Encourage Customer Reviews and Ratings**: Positive customer reviews and high ratings can significantly improve your local search visibility and trustworthiness,

which are important factors for voice search results.

5. **Optimize for Voice-Driven Local Queries**: Anticipate the types of local queries your target audience may use, such as "near me" or "[service] in [location]," and ensure your content is structured to address these queries effectively.

By implementing these local SEO strategies, you can enhance the visibility and relevance of your content in voice search results, particularly for queries with a strong local intent or context.

Optimizing for Different Voice Assistants

While the underlying technology behind voice search is similar across various voice assistants, there may be subtle differences in how each assistant processes and responds to queries. Understanding these differences and optimizing your content accordingly can help improve its performance across multiple voice search platforms.

Understanding Platform-Specific Differences

The major voice assistants, such as Alexa, Siri, Google Assistant, and Cortana, each have their own unique features, capabilities, and user preferences that can impact how your content is perceived and displayed in voice search results.

Some key differences to consider include:

1. **Supported Query Types**: Different voice assistants may have varying capabilities when it comes to understanding and responding to different types of queries, such as informational, transactional, or navigational.
2. **Preferred Response Formats**: Voice assistants may have preferences for the format of the information they provide, such as short, direct answers, summarized information, or more detailed responses.

3. **Integration with Ecosystem**: The integration of a voice assistant with a broader ecosystem of devices, services, and platforms can also influence the way it processes and presents information to users.
4. **User Demographics and Preferences**: The demographics and preferences of a voice assistant's user base may also shape the types of content and information they find most useful and engaging.

By understanding these platform-specific differences, you can tailor your content and optimization strategies to better align with the unique requirements and expectations of each voice assistant.

Optimizing for Multiple Voice Assistants

To ensure your content performs well across a variety of voice search platforms, consider the following optimization strategies:

1. **Conduct Platform-Specific Keyword Research**: Identify the types of queries and phrasing that users of each voice assistant tend to use, and optimize your content accordingly.
2. **Leverage Platform-Specific Features**: Utilize the unique features and capabilities of each voice assistant, such as Alexa Skills or Google Assistant Actions, to enhance the user experience and visibility of your content.
3. **Optimize for Cross-Platform Consistency**: Ensure that the core information and formatting of your content is consistent across different voice search platforms, while still adapting to platform-specific preferences.
4. **Monitor and Analyze Platform Performance**: Track the performance of your content on each voice search platform and make adjustments to your optimization strategies based on the

unique characteristics and behaviors of each user base.

By taking a comprehensive, platform-agnostic approach to voice search optimization, you can maximize the visibility and effectiveness of your content across the diverse and rapidly evolving terrain of voice assistants and voice search technologies.

Technical factors, such as site speed and mobile-friendliness, play a crucial role in voice search optimization. Voice search users expect fast and seamless experiences, and search engines prioritize content that provides a positive user experience, especially on mobile devices.

Ensuring your website is optimized for fast loading times, responsive design, and touch-friendly interactions can significantly improve your chances of performing well in voice search results.

Local SEO is particularly important for voice search, as many voice queries are related to finding local businesses, services, or information. Optimizing your content and website for local search, through tactics like claiming and optimizing your business listings, leveraging location-based keywords, and encouraging customer reviews, can enhance your visibility and relevance in voice search results.

While the underlying technology behind voice search is similar across various voice assistants, there may be subtle differences in how each assistant processes and responds to queries. Understanding these platform-specific differences and optimizing your content accordingly can help improve its performance across multiple voice search platforms.

By addressing these technical optimization factors, you can create a seamless, user-friendly experience for voice search users, while also improving your visibility and relevance in the increasingly competitive voice search terrain.

Chapter 7: Integrating Voice Search into Your Content Strategy

Identifying Voice Search Opportunities

Identifying opportunities to integrate voice search optimization into your content strategy requires a deep understanding of your target audience, their search behaviors, and the types of queries they are likely to use. This process involves analyzing your existing content, conducting in-depth keyword research, and gathering valuable customer insights.

Analyzing Existing Content

The first step in identifying voice search opportunities is to closely examine your existing content and identify areas that can be optimized for voice search. This may involve:

1. **Reviewing Site Analytics**: Analyze your website's search data, including the types of queries that are driving traffic and

engagement, to uncover potential voice search opportunities.

2. **Assessing Content Performance**: Evaluate the performance of your existing content in terms of visibility, relevance, and user engagement to determine which pieces may be well-suited for voice search optimization.

3. **Identifying Knowledge Gaps**: Examine the types of questions, informational needs, or tasks that your current content does not adequately address, and consider how you can create new content to fill those gaps.

4. **Evaluating Content Structure**: Assess the structure and formatting of your existing content to identify areas where improvements can be made to better align with voice search best practices.

By thoroughly analyzing your existing content, you can gain valuable insights into the voice search queries and user behaviors that are most relevant to your business or industry.

Conducting Keyword Research

In addition to analyzing your current content, conducting in-depth keyword research is crucial for identifying voice search opportunities. This research should focus on uncovering the specific types of queries and phrasing that your target audience is likely to use when conducting voice searches.

Some key strategies for voice search keyword research include:

1. **Leveraging Voice Search-Specific Tools**: Utilize specialized keyword research tools, such as Answer the Public or Backlinko's Voice Search Analyzer, to uncover common voice search queries and long-tail keywords.
2. **Analyzing Competitor Data**: Examine the voice search strategies and content of your competitors to identify the types of

queries they are targeting and the opportunities you can capitalize on.
3. **Gathering Customer Insights**: Engage directly with your target audience through surveys, interviews, or online forums to better understand their natural language and the types of questions or commands they are likely to use in voice search.

By combining the insights from your content analysis and comprehensive keyword research, you can develop a clear understanding of the voice search opportunities that are most relevant to your business or industry.

Integrating Customer Insights

Lastly, integrating customer insights and feedback is essential for identifying voice search opportunities that truly resonate with your target audience. This may involve:

1. **Analyzing Customer Support Interactions**: Review the types of questions or issues that customers

regularly bring up in your customer support channels, as these can provide valuable clues about their informational needs and search behaviors.

2. **Gathering User Feedback**: Actively solicit feedback from your customers, either through surveys, user testing, or other engagement channels, to understand their preferences, pain points, and expectations when it comes to voice search.

3. **Monitoring User Behavior**: Closely track and analyze the ways in which your customers interact with your voice search-optimized content, including the types of queries they use and the actions they take in response to your content.

By integrating these customer insights into your voice search opportunity analysis, you can ensure that your content strategy and optimization efforts are truly aligned with the needs and behaviors of your target audience.

Creating a Voice Search Content Plan

Developing a comprehensive voice search content plan involves aligning your content creation, optimization, and distribution efforts with the unique requirements and best practices of voice search. This may include creating new content specifically tailored for voice search, optimizing your existing content, and integrating voice search considerations into your overall content strategy.

Crafting Voice Search-Optimized Content

One of the key components of a voice search content plan is the creation of new content that is specifically designed to meet the needs and expectations of voice search users. This can involve:

1. **Developing Concise, Direct Content:** Focus on creating content that provides clear, concise, and direct answers to the types of queries your target audience is likely to ask via voice search.

2. **Incorporating Conversational Language**: Ensure that the tone and phrasing of your voice search-optimized content aligns with the natural, conversational language used in voice queries.
3. **Structuring for Visibility**: Organize your content in a way that enhances its visibility and relevance in voice search results, such as using clear headings, subheadings, and structured data markup.
4. **Targeting Featured Snippets**: Optimize your content to be selected as a featured snippet, as these are often the preferred response format for voice search users.

By creating content that is specifically tailored to the unique characteristics of voice search, you can improve its discoverability, relevance, and overall performance in voice search results.

Optimizing Existing Content

In addition to crafting new voice search-optimized content, it's also important to review and optimize your existing content to better align with the requirements of voice search. This may involve:

1. **Revisiting Keyword Targeting**: Ensure that your existing content is optimized for the specific keywords and phrases that your target audience is likely to use in voice search queries.
2. **Enhancing Content Structure**: Analyze the structure and formatting of your existing content and make any necessary improvements to better meet the expectations of voice search users.
3. **Integrating Structured Data**: Incorporate schema markup and other structured data elements into your existing content to help search engines better understand and display your information in voice search results.

4. **Improving Mobile-Friendliness**: Evaluate the mobile-responsiveness and performance of your existing content, and make any necessary updates to ensure a seamless experience for voice search users.

By optimizing your existing content for voice search, you can leverage your current assets to enhance their visibility and impact in the voice search terrain.

Integrating Voice Search into Your Overall Content Strategy

To truly maximize the benefits of voice search, it's essential to integrate voice search considerations into your overall content strategy. This may involve:

1. **Aligning Content Goals and KPIs**: Establish clear, voice search-specific goals and key performance indicators (KPIs) that can be used to measure the success of your voice search optimization efforts.

2. **Coordinating Content Creation and Distribution**: Ensure that your voice search-optimized content is seamlessly integrated into your broader content creation and distribution workflows, across various channels and platforms.
3. **Leveraging Voice Search Insights**: Continuously analyze the performance and user feedback of your voice search-optimized content, and use these insights to refine your content strategy and optimization approaches over time.
4. **Exploring Emerging Voice Search Opportunities**: Stay informed about the latest trends and developments in the voice search terrain, and proactively explore new opportunities to leverage voice search as part of your overall content strategy.

By taking a holistic, strategic approach to integrating voice search into your content efforts, you can maximize the impact and long-term success of your voice search optimization initiatives.

Measuring and Tracking Voice Search Performance

Monitoring and analyzing the performance of your voice search-optimized content is crucial for refining your strategy and achieving better results. This involves tracking key metrics, gathering user feedback, and continuously iterating on your approach to voice search optimization.

Tracking Voice Search Metrics

To effectively measure the performance of your voice search-optimized content, focus on tracking the following key metrics:

1. **Voice Search Impressions**: Monitor the number of times your content is displayed as a result in voice search queries, as this can provide insights into its discoverability and relevance.

2. **Voice Search Click-Through Rate (CTR)**: Analyze the rate at which users engage with your voice search-optimized content, as this can indicate the level of user interest and satisfaction.
3. **Voice Search Conversions**: Track the actions taken by users after engaging with your voice search-optimized content, such as making a purchase, filling out a form, or contacting your business.
4. **Featured Snippet Performance**: Closely monitor the performance of your content that is displayed as featured snippets in voice search results, as this can be a crucial indicator of its effectiveness.
5. **User Feedback and Sentiment**: Gather qualitative feedback from users, either directly or through online reviews and surveys, to understand their perceptions and satisfaction with your voice search-optimized content.

By regularly tracking and analyzing these key metrics, you can gain valuable insights into the effectiveness of your voice search optimization efforts and identify areas for improvement.

Refining Your Voice Search Strategy

The data and insights gathered from your voice search performance tracking should be used to continuously refine and optimize your content strategy. This may involve:

1. **Identifying Top-Performing Content**: Analyze the voice search metrics to determine which of your content pieces are resonating most with your target audience, and use these insights to inform your future content creation and optimization efforts.
2. **Addressing Performance Gaps**: Identify any areas where your voice search-optimized content is underperforming, and use these insights to make targeted improvements, such as

enhancing content structure, adjusting keyword targeting, or improving mobile-friendliness.

3. **Experimenting with New Approaches**: Continuously test and explore new voice search optimization tactics, such as leveraging different content formats, trying alternative keyword strategies, or adapting to changes in voice search algorithms and user behaviors.

4. **Collaborating with Cross-Functional Teams**: Engage with other teams, such as SEO, marketing, and customer experience, to ensure that your voice search optimization efforts are aligned with and supported by your broader digital strategy.

By regularly monitoring, analyzing, and iterating on your voice search optimization efforts, you can ensure that your content strategy remains responsive, effective, and aligned with the evolving needs and preferences of your target audience.

Integrating voice search into your content strategy requires a multi-faceted approach that involves identifying voice search opportunities, creating a comprehensive voice search content plan, and continuously measuring and refining your performance.

Identifying voice search opportunities starts with a deep understanding of your target audience, their search behaviors, and the types of queries they are likely to use. This process involves analyzing your existing content, conducting in-depth keyword research, and integrating valuable customer insights.

Developing a voice search content plan entails aligning your content creation, optimization, and distribution efforts with the unique requirements and best practices of voice search. This may include creating new content specifically tailored for voice search, optimizing your existing content, and seamlessly integrating voice search considerations into your overall content strategy.

Measuring and tracking the performance of your voice search-optimized content is crucial for refining your strategy and achieving better results. This involves tracking key metrics, such as voice search impressions, click-through rates, and conversions, as well as gathering user feedback and insights to continuously improve your approach.

By taking a comprehensive, strategic approach to integrating voice search into your content efforts, you can enhance the discoverability, relevance, and overall impact of your content in the rapidly evolving voice search terrain.

Chapter 8: Voice Search and Emerging Technologies

Voice Search and the Internet of Things (IoT)

As the Internet of Things (IoT) continues to evolve, the integration of voice search technology into various connected devices, such as smart home appliances, vehicles, and wearables, is expected to grow. Understanding the implications of this convergence and how it can impact your content optimization efforts is important for staying ahead of the curve.

The Rise of Voice-Enabled IoT Devices

The proliferation of IoT devices, which are connected to the internet and capable of exchanging data, has opened up new frontiers for voice search integration. Devices like smart speakers, smart home hubs, in-car infotainment systems, and even wearable technologies are increasingly incorporating voice search capabilities, allowing users to control, interact with, and access information through voice commands.

Some key drivers behind the rise of voice-enabled IoT devices include:

1. **Hands-Free Convenience**: Voice control provides a more natural and convenient way for users to interact with their connected devices, particularly in situations where manual inputs are impractical or unsafe, such as when driving or multitasking.
2. **Seamless User Experience**: The integration of voice search into IoT devices creates a more seamless, interconnected user experience, where users can easily access information, control their environment, and perform tasks across multiple devices and platforms.
3. **Advancements in Natural Language Processing**: Improvements in natural language processing (NLP) and speech

recognition technologies have enabled more accurate and natural-sounding voice interactions, driving greater adoption and use of voice-enabled IoT devices.

As the IoT ecosystem continues to expand, the integration of voice search capabilities into an increasingly diverse range of connected devices will become more prevalent, presenting both opportunities and challenges for content creators and businesses.

Optimizing Content for Voice-Enabled IoT

To effectively optimize your content for the emerging terrain of voice-enabled IoT devices, consider the following strategies:

1. **Understand Device-Specific Capabilities**: Familiarize yourself with the unique features, capabilities, and constraints of the various IoT devices that are likely to be used for voice search, such as smart speakers, in-car systems, or wearables. This will help you tailor your

content and optimization approaches accordingly.

2. **Prioritize Concise and Actionable Content**: Given the often hands-free and multitasking nature of voice interactions with IoT devices, focus on creating content that is highly concise, direct, and actionable, providing users with the most relevant and useful information at a glance.

3. **Optimize for Relevant Queries**: Identify the types of voice search queries that users are likely to make when interacting with IoT devices in different contexts, such as smart home management, in-vehicle information, or health and fitness tracking, and optimize your content accordingly.

4. **Leverage Multimodal Experiences**: Explore opportunities to integrate your voice search-optimized content with other modalities, such as visual or haptic feedback, to create more engaging and

comprehensive user experiences across IoT devices.

5. **Collaborate with IoT Device Manufacturers**: Establish partnerships and collaborations with IoT device manufacturers to ensure your content is properly integrated, discoverable, and optimized for their specific voice search capabilities and user interfaces.

By staying ahead of the curve in the evolving IoT terrain and adapting your content optimization strategies accordingly, you can position your content for success in this emerging voice search-driven ecosystem.

Voice Commerce and Voice Shopping

Voice-enabled commerce, or voice commerce, is another emerging trend that is shaping the future of voice search. As more consumers adopt voice-based shopping and purchasing behaviors, content creators and businesses must adapt their strategies to cater to this new channel, optimizing their content and user experiences for voice-driven transactions.

The Rise of Voice Commerce

The rise of voice commerce can be attributed to several factors, including the growing adoption of voice-enabled devices, the increasing consumer preference for hands-free and on-the-go shopping experiences, and the ongoing advancements in natural language processing and voice recognition technologies.

Some key developments driving the growth of voice commerce include:

1. **Proliferation of Smart Speakers**: The widespread adoption of smart speakers, such as Amazon Echo and Google Home, has made voice-based shopping more accessible and convenient for consumers.
2. **Integration with Voice Assistants**: The integration of voice commerce capabilities with virtual assistants, like Alexa and Google Assistant, has further expanded

the reach and functionality of voice-based shopping experiences.

3. **Expansion of Voice-Enabled Ecommerce**: Major e-commerce platforms and retailers are increasingly incorporating voice search and voice ordering capabilities into their customer experiences, making it easier for consumers to discover, research, and purchase products using their voice.

As voice commerce continues to gain traction, content creators and businesses must adapt their strategies to cater to this growing segment of consumers who are embracing voice-based shopping and purchasing behaviors.

Optimizing for Voice Commerce

To effectively optimize your content and user experiences for voice commerce, consider the following strategies:

1. **Facilitate Voice-Driven Product Discovery**: Ensure that your product

information, descriptions, and reviews are structured in a way that makes it easy for voice search users to discover and evaluate your offerings through voice-based queries.

2. **Enable Voice-Based Transactions**: Integrate voice-enabled ordering and checkout capabilities into your e-commerce platform, allowing customers to seamlessly complete purchases using voice commands.

3. **Provide Conversational Product Guidance**: Offer voice-based product recommendations, personalized assistance, and detailed information to help customers navigate and make informed purchasing decisions through voice interactions.

4. **Optimize for Voice-Specific Queries**: Identify the types of voice-based queries that your customers are likely to use when searching for and purchasing products,

and optimize your content and search strategies accordingly.

5. **Leverage Multimodal Experiences**: Explore opportunities to combine voice-based interactions with other modalities, such as visual displays or haptic feedback, to create more engaging and immersive voice commerce experiences.

6. **Analyze Voice Commerce Performance**: Continuously monitor and analyze the performance of your voice commerce-optimized content and user experiences, using relevant metrics to inform your ongoing optimization efforts.

By adapting your content and user experience strategies to the unique requirements and preferences of voice commerce, you can position your business to capitalize on this rapidly growing and evolving segment of the digital terrain.

Artificial Intelligence and Voice Search Evolution

The rapid advancements in artificial intelligence (AI) and machine learning are expected to drive further improvements and innovations in voice search technology. Understanding the potential impact of these emerging technologies on voice search and content optimization can help you future-proof your strategies and stay ahead of the competition.

The Role of AI in Voice Search

Artificial intelligence and machine learning have become integral to the development and evolution of voice search technology. These advanced technologies are powering the core capabilities that enable voice search, including:

1. **Natural Language Processing (NLP)**: AI-powered NLP algorithms are responsible for understanding the semantic meaning, intent, and context behind voice-based queries, allowing voice

search systems to provide more accurate and relevant responses.

2. **Speech Recognition**: Machine learning models are continuously improving the accuracy and robustness of speech recognition, enabling voice search systems to more reliably convert spoken language into machine-readable text.

3. **Personalization and Contextual Awareness**: AI-driven personalization and context-aware algorithms are enhancing the ability of voice search systems to tailor their responses to the individual user's preferences, location, and past interactions.

4. **Multimodal Interactions**: The integration of AI and machine learning is enabling voice search systems to seamlessly incorporate and coordinate multiple input and output modalities, such as visual, haptic, and conversational interfaces.

As AI and machine learning continue to advance, the capabilities and performance of voice search technology are expected to undergo significant improvements, with far-reaching implications for content optimization and user experiences.

The Future of Voice Search and Content Optimization

The ongoing evolution of AI and machine learning in voice search technology will likely have a profound impact on the way content creators and businesses approach voice search optimization. Some key trends and considerations include:

1. **Hyper-Personalization**: As voice search systems become more adept at understanding individual user preferences and contexts, content optimization strategies will need to adapt to deliver highly personalized and tailored experiences.

2. **Multimodal Optimization**: The integration of voice search with other input and output modalities, such as visual, haptic, and gestural interfaces, will require content creators to think holistically about optimizing their content for seamless, cross-channel experiences.

3. **Anticipatory Content Delivery**: Advances in AI-powered predictive analytics and intent recognition may enable voice search systems to proactively surface and deliver the most relevant content to users, even before they explicitly ask for it.

4. **Conversational Content Creation**: As voice search systems become more adept at understanding and engaging in natural, conversational dialogues, content creators may need to rethink their approach to crafting content that can fluidly respond to user queries and follow-up questions.

5. **Automated Content Optimization:** The increasing sophistication of AI and machine learning algorithms may lead to the development of automated content optimization tools and services that can continuously analyze, optimize, and refine content for voice search performance.

By staying informed about the evolving role of AI and machine learning in voice search technology, content creators and businesses can better future-proof their strategies, adapt to emerging trends, and position their content for long-term success in the rapidly changing voice search terrain.

As the Internet of Things (IoT) continues to evolve, the integration of voice search technology into various connected devices, such as smart home appliances, vehicles, and wearables, is expected to grow. Understanding the implications of this convergence and adapting your content optimization strategies accordingly will be crucial for staying ahead of the curve.

Voice-enabled commerce, or voice commerce, is another emerging trend that is shaping the future of voice search. As more consumers adopt voice-based shopping and purchasing behaviors, content creators and businesses must adapt their strategies to cater to this new channel, optimizing their content and user experiences for voice-driven transactions.

The rapid advancements in artificial intelligence (AI) and machine learning are also expected to drive further improvements and innovations in voice search technology. Understanding the potential impact of these emerging technologies on voice search and content optimization can help you future-proof your strategies and stay ahead of the competition.

By staying informed and proactive in addressing the evolving terrain of voice search and emerging technologies, content creators and businesses can position themselves for long-term success in this rapidly changing and increasingly voice-driven digital environment.

Conclusion

Recap of Key Points

In this comprehensive guide, we have explored the various aspects of mastering voice search content optimization, covering a wide range of topics that are crucial for success in the rapidly evolving voice search terrain.

We began by examining the rise of voice search and its growing importance in the digital world. We discussed the key players in the voice search market, including Amazon Alexa, Google Assistant, Apple Siri, and Microsoft Cortana, and the unique features and capabilities that each platform offers. We also explored the different types of voice search queries, from informational and navigational to transactional and local, and how understanding user behaviors and preferences is essential for effective voice search optimization.

Next, we delved into the underlying technology that powers voice search, including natural language processing (NLP), speech recognition, and the role of machine learning and artificial intelligence. We explored the ranking factors that search engines use to determine the most relevant and optimal voice search results, with a focus on factors such as conciseness, relevance, and the ability to provide a direct answer.

Moving on, we discussed the importance of keyword research for voice search optimization. We highlighted the significance of long-tail keywords and conversational phrases, and the various tools and techniques that can be used to identify the types of queries that your target audience is likely to use when conducting voice searches.

Structuring and formatting your content for voice search was another key focus area. We covered best practices for organizing your content in a clear and concise manner, utilizing relevant headers and subheadings, and incorporating structured data and schema markup to enhance the visibility and relevance of your content in voice search results.

Writing for voice search was also a crucial topic in our exploration. We emphasized the importance of adopting a natural and conversational tone, crafting concise and direct answers, and framing your content around common voice search queries, such as questions and commands.

Technical optimization, including the impact of site speed, mobile-friendliness, and local SEO, was another essential component of our discussion. We also explored the nuances of optimizing for different voice assistants and the importance of understanding platform-specific differences.

Finally, we delved into the integration of voice search into your overall content strategy, covering the process of identifying voice search opportunities, creating a comprehensive voice search content plan, and measuring and tracking the performance of your voice search-optimized content.

Throughout this guide, we also examined the emerging trends and technologies that are shaping the future of voice search, including the integration of voice search into the Internet of Things (IoT), the rise of voice commerce, and the impact of artificial intelligence and machine learning on the evolution of voice search technology.

Future of Voice Search and Content Optimization

As voice search technology continues to evolve and become more widespread, the importance of optimizing your content for this growing search channel will only increase. By staying proactive and adapting your strategies to the changing terrain, you can position your content for success in the voice search era and capitalize on the tremendous opportunities it offers.

Some of the key trends and developments that are likely to shape the future of voice search and content optimization include:

1. **Hyper-Personalization**: As AI and machine learning capabilities advance, voice search systems will become increasingly adept at understanding individual user preferences, contexts, and behaviors, enabling the delivery of highly personalized and tailored content experiences.
2. **Multimodal Optimization**: The integration of voice search with other input and output modalities, such as visual, haptic, and gestural interfaces, will require content creators to think holistically about optimizing their content for seamless, cross-channel experiences.
3. **Anticipatory Content Delivery**: Advancements in predictive analytics and intent recognition may enable voice search systems to proactively surface and deliver

the most relevant content to users, even before they explicitly ask for it.

4. **Conversational Content Creation**: As voice search systems become more adept at understanding and engaging in natural, conversational dialogues, content creators may need to rethink their approach to crafting content that can fluidly respond to user queries and follow-up questions.

5. **Automated Content Optimization**: The increasing sophistication of AI and machine learning algorithms may lead to the development of automated content optimization tools and services that can continuously analyze, optimize, and refine content for voice search performance.

By staying informed about these emerging trends and proactively adapting your strategies to the changing voice search terrain, you can position your content for long-term success and capitalize on the tremendous growth opportunities that this dynamic search channel has to offer.

Final Thoughts and Recommendations

Mastering voice search content optimization is a strategic imperative for businesses and content creators in the modern digital terrain. By understanding the unique characteristics of voice search, leveraging best practices, and staying ahead of emerging trends, you can enhance the discoverability, relevance, and performance of your content, ultimately driving greater engagement, traffic, and conversions.

To achieve success in the voice search era, we recommend the following key strategies:

1. **Develop a Comprehensive Voice Search Optimization Strategy**: Integrate voice search considerations into your overall content strategy, aligning your content creation, optimization, and distribution efforts with the unique

requirements and best practices of voice search.

2. **Focus on User-Centric Experiences**: Prioritize the needs and preferences of your target audience, crafting content that provides concise, direct, and conversational answers to their voice-based queries.

3. **Leverage Data and Analytics**: Continuously monitor and analyze the performance of your voice search-optimized content, using the insights to refine your strategies and adapt to the evolving voice search terrain.

4. **Stay Ahead of Emerging Trends**: Keep a close eye on the latest developments in voice search technology, including the integration of AI, IoT, and voice commerce, and proactively explore new opportunities to leverage these emerging trends.

5. **Collaborate and Innovate**: Engage with cross-functional teams, industry experts, and technology partners to stay at the forefront of voice search innovation and explore new ways to deliver exceptional voice search experiences for your audience.

By embracing these strategies and continuously evolving your voice search optimization efforts, you can position your content for long-term success and thrive in the rapidly changing and increasingly voice-driven digital ecosystem.

Resources

Glossary of Voice Search Terms

1. **Natural Language Processing (NLP)**: The ability of a computer program to understand human language as it is spoken and written.
2. **Speech Recognition**: The ability of a computer program to identify words and

phrases in spoken language and convert them to a machine-readable format.
3. **Featured Snippet**: A short, concise answer to a user's query that is displayed prominently at the top of the search results.
4. **Knowledge Panel**: A summary of information about a specific topic or entity, often displayed on the right-hand side of search results.
5. **Long-Tail Keywords**: Less common, more specific keywords and phrases that tend to have lower search volume but higher relevance and conversion potential.
6. **Voice Commerce**: The ability to purchase products or services using voice-enabled devices and virtual assistants.

Recommended Tools and Resources

Keyword Research Tools:

- Google Keyword Planner
- SEMrush

- Ahrefs
- Moz Keyword Explorer

Voice Search Optimization Tools:

- Answer the Public
- Backlinko Voice Search Optimization Analyzer
- Yoast Voice Search Optimization

Voice Search Reporting and Analytics:

- Google Search Console
- Google Analytics Voice Search Reports

By leveraging these resources and continuously expanding your knowledge and skills in voice search optimization, you can position your content for long-term success and thrive in the rapidly evolving voice search terrain.

ABOUT THE AUTHOR

Harrell Howard is a versatile author with a passion for writing on technology, fiction, kids' books, and money matters. His work encompasses thought-provoking technology articles, enchanting fiction tales, captivating children's books, and insightful money-related pieces. With a commitment to research and a knack for storytelling, Harrell's writing resonates with readers of all ages, leaving a lasting impact on the literary world.

www.ingramcontent.com/pod-product-compliance
Lightning Source LLC
Chambersburg PA
CBHW050110230526
45470CB00004B/1763